Alta Community School District
Elementary Library

D1154551

2641

597.96 Hess, Lilo
H
      That snake in the
      grass

$12.95

	DATE	
SEP 27 1991		
OCT 07 1991		
NOV 5 1992		
DEC 15 1992		
OCT 28 1993		
NOV 24 1993		
OCT 13 '94		
OCT 28 '96		
'96		

DISCARD

2641

ALTA COMM SCHOOL DISTRICT
101 W 5TH ST
ALTA, IOWA
51002

   08/02/90   12.95

              694285   02783

© THE BAKER & TAYLOR CO.

THAT SNAKE
IN THE GRASS

THAT SNAKE IN THE GRASS

Lilo Hess

Charles Scribner's Sons • New York

2641- Baker Taylor- 1990

*The snake on page 1 is an African Ball Python,
and the snake on page 2 is a Pine Snake.*

Copyright © 1987 by Lilo Hess

All rights reserved. No part of this book may be reproduced or
transmitted in any form or by any means, electronic or mechanical,
including photocopying, recording, or by any information storage and
retrieval system, without permission in writing from the Publisher.

Charles Scribner's Sons Books for Young Readers
Macmillan Publishing Company
866 Third Avenue, New York, NY 10022
Collier Macmillan Canada, Inc.

Printed in the United States of America
First Edition   10 9 8 7 6 5 4 3 2

Library of Congress Cataloging-in-Publication Data
Hess, Lilo.   That snake in the grass.
Includes index.
Summary: A discussion of snakes in the wild and at home as pets.
1. Snakes—Juvenile literature.   2. Snakes as pets—Juvenile literature.
[1. Snakes.   2. Snakes as pets]   I. Title.
QL666.06H58   1987   597.96   86-24826
ISBN 0-684-18591-1

Illustration by Gloria Stevens

Strange stories have always been told about snakes, more so than any other animal. Should we believe them? Can a snake really put its tail into its mouth and roll along like a hoop? Can a snake sneak into a barn and drink milk directly from a cow's udder? Is it true that a snake won't cross a rope made out of horsehair? Will you regain your youth if you eat a snake? The answer to all of these questions is *no*, but fears and superstitions about snakes survive and are passed on from generation to generation. Even in our everyday language, expressions of loathing

5

and distrust refer to snakes. We call a person we don't like a "snake in the grass" or a "low-down snake," or we claim that someone who lies "speaks with a forked tongue."

AFRICAN BALL PYTHON

Ever since the beginning of recorded history the snake has been hated, and many myths have grown around it. The Bible tells us that a snake tempted Adam and Eve to eat the fruit from the forbidden tree of knowledge in the Garden of Eden, and that God punished it by making it crawl forever on its belly. Some African tribes still believe that a snake in their home or yard is a dead relative who has returned. American Hopi Indians performed a four-day snake dance as a prayer for rain. The

snake charmers of India, called *fakirs*, carry about Cobras, one of the world's most poisonous snakes, in baskets to perform wherever crowds gather. They tell their audiences that the snake is lulled and hypnotized by the sweet music they play on a gourd pipe, but it is not the music that makes the snake rear up and sway rhythmically back and forth. A snake cannot hear; it follows the motion of the fakir and his pipe, bending and twisting as the snake charmer moves his body.

If we look at a snake closely and without prejudice, all we see is a sluggish, small-brained, slender-bodied, limbless animal that is very good at surviving against many odds. It is very useful to farmers because it consumes many harmful rodents.

Alta Community School District
Elementary Library

There are nearly 30,000 species of snakes in the world. They belong to a group of animals called reptiles and are descendants of lizards.

It is said snakes lost their limbs about 100 million years ago, but nobody knows exactly how it happened. There are two theories. One is that legless lizards just changed gradually into snakes. The other idea is that there were burrowing lizards who lived underground and whose limbs became smaller and smaller until they disappeared entirely. Later these creatures moved above ground, managed to survive despite their limbless condition, and became the snakes we know today.

PYTHON

All snakes can swim, many can climb, and most move swiftly over all kinds of terrain. Although they can move very fast, snakes cannot outrun a human. Snakes are also called serpents, which means "crawling animals." The crawling, sliding motion of snakes often scares and repulses people.

11

A snake moves with the help of strong muscles and the scales on its belly. Those scales are attached to the body skin at one end and are free on the other end. That way they can grip the rough ground and push the snake forward. Some species move forward in an S-shaped pattern. These gripping scales and muscles also make it possible for the snake to climb into a tree or move easily through thick underbrush. On a glass or other very smooth surface a snake cannot move well. In water, a wiggling motion helps the snake to swim.

Some snakes still have undeveloped "hind legs" in the form of two very tiny spurs, one on each side of the pelvic region. Anacondas, Boas, and Pythons have visible spurs, but do not use them for locomotion. They sometimes use them to stimulate the opposite sex.

There are several advantages to not having limbs. Snakes can go into extremely small holes or through very narrow cracks or rock cavities. They can slide under tight ledges and hide under flat stones. Animals with limbs could never do that.

Photo by Susan Brooks

Snakes come in all sizes. The smallest are probably the Worm Snakes and the Miter Snakes. Both live underground and are wormlike animals that get about eight inches long. The largest snakes are the South American Anacondas and the Pythons of Africa, India, and other Old-World tropics. They attain a length of over twenty feet.

13

Scientists have put snakes into various family groups. The four best-known groups are:

PYTHON

The Boidae to which Pythons, Boas, and others belong. They are constrictors, meaning that they kill prey by stopping its respiration and heartbeat. They are nonpoisonous.

BLUE INDIGO

The Colubridae is the largest family of snakes, and most are nonpoisonous. Almost all the snakes that make good pets belong to this group.

COBRA

The Elapidae is the family to which Cobras, Mambas, Adders, and others belong. They are extremely poisonous.

The Crotalidae is mostly a family of poisonous snakes found in North and South America that includes Pit Vipers, Rattlesnakes, Copperheads, Moccasins, Cottonmouths, and others.

COPPERHEAD

Snakes do not hear the way we, and most other animals, do; they have no external ear openings. However, they can feel vibration through the skull bone. They have fairly good vision and might even see some color. Snakes stare unblinkingly at their world. They have no eyelids and can never close their eyes, even when they sleep. A clear lens covers and protects the eye.

There are some lizards that have no limbs and look very much like snakes. The Glass Snake Lizard is one of them. A sure way

to tell a lizard from a snake is to look at its eyes. All lizards have eyelids and can close them at will. They also have external ear openings, one on each side of the head, as you can see in the picture of the iguana.

In addition to regular eyesight, snakes have a remarkable organ called the Jacobson's organ, which acts almost like a third eye. This organ, located on each side of the snake's snout, contains very sensitive nerve endings that are connected by ducts to an opening in the roof of the mouth. When the snake's forked tongue flicks rapidly in and out, it is actually picking up tiny particles from the air and taking them to the roof of the mouth. From there the air samples are sent to the nerve endings to be analyzed. This way the snake can recognize a mate, find out what the ground and atmospheric conditions are, or locate food or enemies.

16

Like other animals, snakes have nostrils and can smell fairly well. But some of the poisonous snakes like the Pit Vipers and their relatives get extra help in locating their food from another strange organ, the pit organ, which is located halfway between the eye and the nostril on each side of the snake's head. It contains nerves that sense heat waves radiating from warm-blooded animals. The nerves send the message to the brain, and the snake knows exactly where and at what distance a prey animal is hiding. This is very useful, especially when hunting in the dark. A few of the nonpoisonous Boas and Pythons also have heat-detectors, but they are located near the mouth.

Snakes are cold-blooded animals, meaning that, unlike humans and other warm-blooded creatures, they have no mechanism for maintaining a constant body temperature. Snakes cannot tolerate temperatures too hot or too cold. No snakes live where the subsoil is always frozen. The reason there are no snakes in Ireland is not because Saint Patrick drove them out of the country, but because about 10,000 years ago, during the last glacial epoch, it was much too cold for snakes to survive. After the ice receded, the waters rose and Ireland became separated from England before any snakes could return. Many oceanic islands have no snakes, either. Hawaii, for instance, has only one small, harmless species that probably was brought in by accident.

To warm themselves, snakes bask in the sun. We can see them on rocks, along roadsides, on woodpiles, and in other open spots that get full sunlight. Snakes are active only between 60° and 104° F (15° to 40° C). If it is too hot, they must seek cooler, shaded places. To keep from freezing in the winter, they go into caves and deep crevices, under rocks, or into dens that have been made and abandoned by mammals. Several snakes might den together, probably for warmth. In the northern United States snakes are active and visible only in the spring and fall, but farther south they stay active most of the year.

RING-NECK SNAKES AND MILK SNAKE

Snakes have to be warm to be hungry. A cold snake will not eat. People are often repulsed because snakes swallow their food whole and sometimes alive, but most snakes kill their prey before eating it. In captivity they sometimes accept dead rats or mice, or strips of meat or fish. The bigger the snake, the larger the animal it hunts. Tiny snakes eat insects, worms, or baby mice. A very large snake could eat a gazelle. Most snakes are very specialized in their food habits, making them hard to feed in captivity.

There are snakes that eat only cold-blooded prey, such as frogs, lizards, or other snakes. The Hog-Nosed Snake, for instance, seldom eats anything other than toads. Snakes can go for a long time—even several months—without food. They are formidable hunters. Some snakes go out and stalk and catch their

BLUE INDIGO

food, while others lie and wait patiently until a meal walks by. Sometimes the victim gets away, like the gecko in the picture, who left only a piece of its tail for the snake's dinner.

21

VINE SNAKE

PYTHON

Snakes kill only when hungry and never harm an animal when they are not ready to eat. A rabbit that had been placed into the zoo cage of a large Python who was not hungry hopped over the snake without fear and lay down to rest alongside it. However, when the Python is ready to eat, it will move like lightning, throwing its body-coils over the victim, cutting off its air supply, and killing it within seconds.

Some snakes drag their fresh-killed prey up a tree or onto a branch to consume it leisurely. The Boa in the picture killed the rat on the ground and consumed it while suspended from a broken branch. Other snakes both kill and consume their prey aloft.

BOA

In captivity, some snakes, such as the various kinds of King Snakes in the picture, sometimes get greedy when they have the chance to catch more than one mouse at a time. They are holding one in their coils while eating another.

CALIFORNIA KING SNAKES

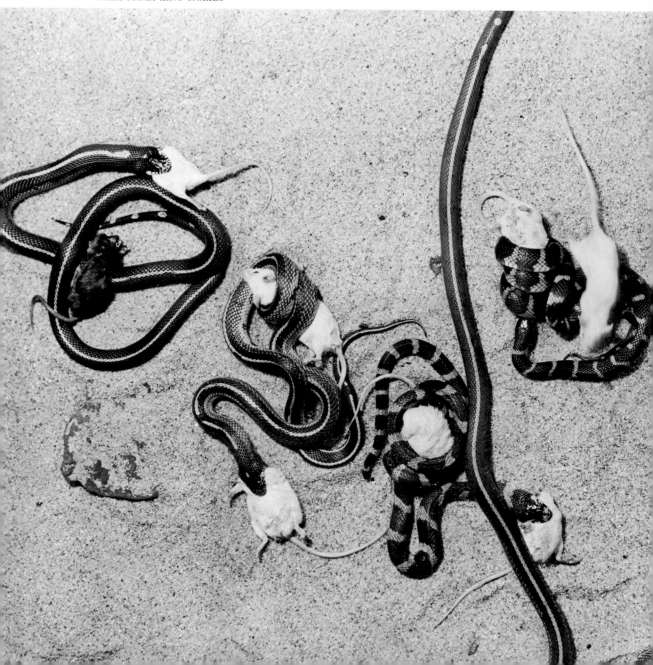

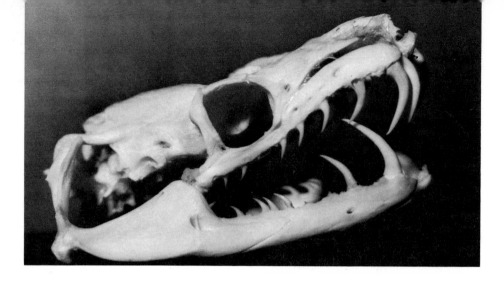

All snakes have rows of sharp pointed teeth that are curved backward. They do not use their teeth for chewing food, but for grabbing and holding, so that the prey can be swallowed easier. All snakes can grow new teeth to replace broken or worn-out ones.

Poisonous snakes use their venom to kill or to immobilize their victims before eating them. One group of poisonous snakes, to which Rattlesnakes, Copperheads, and Vipers belong, have a pair of hollow fangs in the front of the upper jaw through which venom is injected into the prey. These Vipers can also fold their fangs back up to the roof of the mouth when not in use, and so they are called movable fangs. Other snakes, like the Cobras, Mambas, or Coral Snakes, have immovable fangs, which means that the fangs always stay in the same position. Some tropical poisonous snakes called the rear-fanged snakes, only a few species of which are present in the United States, have two or three grooved teeth in the back of the upper jaw. The grooves guide the poison into the victim. The Mexican Vine Snake, the Boomslang of Africa, and the Cat-Eyed Snake of southern Texas belong to this group.

Poisonous snakes have different kinds of venom, but all work quickly and are very potent. Not all poisons are strong enough to hurt a human being, but snake bites should be taken seriously and attended to as quickly as possible. The Cobra's venom paralyzes its victims by damaging the central nervous system, while the poison of Rattlers and their kind kills by destroying body tissues.

But snake venom also works to man's advantage. The venom is extracted from snakes and manufactured into counteragents called antivenins. Because the venom varies from species to species, several types are collected, and the mixture is manufactured into the product used for treating snake bites.

Snakes bite only as a last resort, when they are cornered and cannot get away, or when stepped upon. Their first impulse is to flee. Many give ample warning before they strike. The Rattler's tail, for instance, makes a loud noise as the animal vibrates it.

The Cobra, when it is frightened or angry, rears up, spreads its hood, and hisses, and some species even spit as a warning. It seems the snake hopes that by looking fierce and big, the enemy might go away. Striking and biting might or might not follow. The Cobra can flatten and enlarge its neck and, with the help of muscles that raise the long frontal ribs forward, can form the hood for which it is famous.

Many snakes give off evil-smelling musk to protect themselves, but if they are handled often in captivity, they will lose their fear and stop expelling their musk. Some snakes advertise that they are dangerous by sporting very bright colors, while others, like the Copperheads, have colors that blend in so well with their surroundings that an enemy might not see them. Harmless snakes often are look-alikes of a dangerous species,

COBRA   COPPERHEAD

although scientists do not know why this should be so. But this bluff seems to be effective for the snake's survival.

The master of deception is undoubtedly the Hog-Nosed Snake. This North American reptile is greatly feared because of the ferocious display it puts on when startled or attacked. It raises up like a Cobra, hisses and puffs, and even spreads its neck to make it look like a hood. Because of this performance it is often called a Puff Adder or Blow Adder. Its breath is mistakenly believed to be filled with poisonous fumes. But even

Alta Community School District
Elementary Library

when the Hog-Nosed Snake makes forward stabbing motions, it keeps its mouth closed and never bites.

If all this display fails to scare the enemy away, the Hog-Nosed Snake will then go into its best act. It pushes itself over on its back with the help of its head and strong body muscles. Then it opens its mouth wide, lets its tongue dangle out, and remains motionless, playing dead. One can even pick it up and it will remain motionless on its back in the hand. If undisturbed it will right itself after several minutes and go about its business. The only flaw in this performance is that when turned over on its belly, it will quickly flop back into the belly-up dead position. There are several other kinds of snakes that pretend to be

dead to escape an enemy, but none are better actors than the Hog-Nosed Snake.

The main enemies of snakes are weasels, some hawks, a bird called the roadrunner, other snakes, and man. The Indian mongoose, a weasel-like mammal that ranges through Africa, Asia, and Malaysia, became famous because it kills and eats the deadly Cobra. It also eats birds, rodents, and other reptiles. It is a myth that the mongoose is immune to the Cobra's poisonous bite, but it is extremely quick and fearless and seems to know how to avoid the snake's fangs.

From time to time one finds a transparent empty snake skin in bushes, flowerbeds, woods, or any other place that might be home for a snake. Snakes can grow a new skin directly underneath their old one. Every few months, when the new skin is fully developed, the old skin starts to look dull. The snake's eyes take on a cloudy appearance, and it loses its appetite. Some snakes like to soak in the water at this time. Then the snake rubs its mouth and chin against rough surfaces to loosen the skin and work it over its head and eyes. Finally it succeeds in slipping the old skin off like a glove. The transparent old skin is left behind, and a sparkling fresh and bright-colored one adorns the snake. It glistens and looks shiny as if the snake were wet. But all snakes feel dry, even soft and silky, to the touch.

INTERGRADE RAT SNAKES

Different species of snakes have different ways of wooing a female, but most of them start with nudging, pursuing, and rubbing and with the male twitching his tail. The male then investigates the female with his tongue and by gliding over her. For a while their bodies travel in a parallel pattern, then the male twists his body around the female and keeps his chin close to her neck.

Some snakes give birth to living young, others lay eggs. The female of the egg-laying variety searches for a secluded spot about three to six weeks after mating, depending on the species. To the female a patch of sandy soil, dry leaves, or a shallow depression under a stone or under a piece of tree bark that has fallen to the ground might look like a safe place to deposit her eggs.

BLACK SNAKE EGGS

BLACK SNAKE

Small snakes lay eight to fifteen elongated, rubbery-shelled, white- or cream-colored eggs. Larger snakes may lay many more eggs. Some species of snakes hatch after about one week, others take twelve weeks or more. The baby snake cuts a slit into the rubbery shell with its egg tooth, a tiny sharp toothlike growth on the front of the upper jaw. It falls off a day or two after hatching. Some babies emerge quickly after they have cut the opening into the shell, others take their time. They may remain in the egg for another day, but they look out frequently as if surveying their new world. The female snake usually never sees her offspring; her duty ends after the eggs have been deposited. There are a few exceptions, however. Some of the Cobras build nests, and the male and female guard the eggs. Some Pythons can raise their body temperature during this time to help incubate the eggs, but as soon as those little snakes hatch, they are on their own.

34

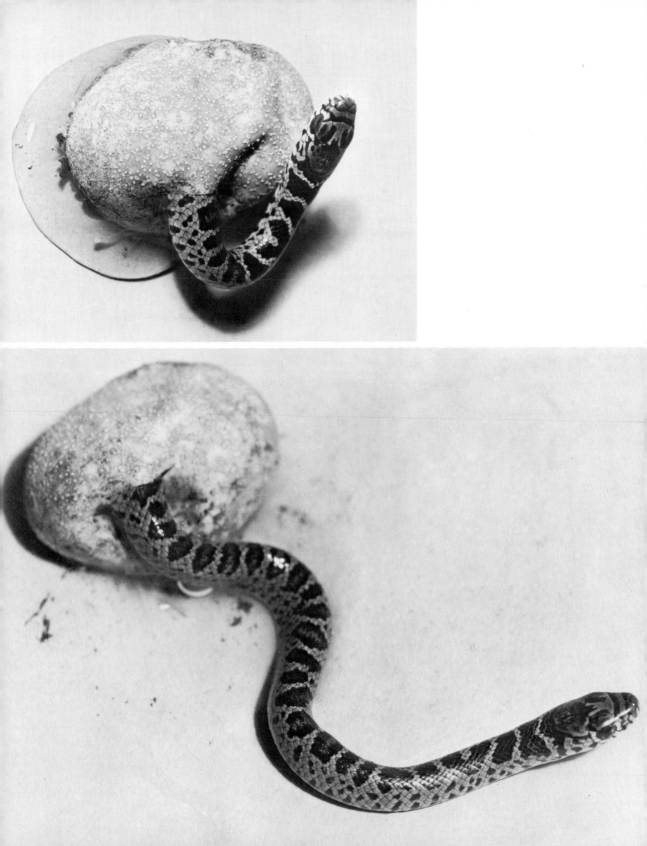

RED-BELLIED WATER SNAKE

Snakes that give birth to living young also leave them right after birth. The number of baby snakes that are born to a female varies with the size and species. Some snakes have only one to eight young ones, others give birth to five to eighteen, and the Eastern Garter Snakes have records of eighty-five to eighty-nine babies.

NEWBORN GARTER SNAKES

Snakes are very popular pets. But can one really love a snake? They do not have the personality of a dog or cat, nor do they show any affection. However, they do get tame and relax when handled. They are quiet pets and don't require the constant care and time other pets need. They can live in relatively small quarters and are clean and almost odorless. If someone is allergic to fur or feathers, a snake might be the answer. The main problem in keeping a snake as a pet is getting the right food for it and overcoming the possible aversions of friends and family members.

CORN SNAKE

KING SNAKE

CORN SNAKE

Which one of the many snakes to keep as a pet is a matter of taste and availability. Most important is that the animal can adjust to captivity and become tame. Adjusting does not mean only that the snake gets used to its cage but also that it eats. Since snakes have such specialized needs for food, it often is very hard to get the right kind for them. The food must be available at all times and not subject to seasonal changes. A snake that eats insects, worms, or small reptiles seems easy to

38

feed during the summer months, but in cold climates these foods will not be available all year round. The same goes for food animals such as frogs or fish.

Scientific or biological supply houses often sell crickets, frogs, small fish, snails, and worms, which some of the smaller snakes might eat. Make sure before you get the snake that those food animals can be shipped during the winter months. If you are lucky enough to have a little snake that eats earthworms, you can grow those easily yourself. The snake might also learn to take thin strips of fish or meat, which can be kept frozen until needed. Although snakes can go long stretches without a meal, they should eat about once a week.

Snakes that eat mice or rats or other small mammals might eventually be trained to eat dead ones, or even a piece of meat that has been rubbed against a rodent. But most of these snakes will need to kill the prey themselves. You can buy mice or rats from laboratories and pet stores, or you can breed them yourself.

Leave the mouse or rat in the cage with the snake for a few hours. If it is not eaten, remove it and offer it again the next day. If the rodent is left too long in the cage with the snake, it might nibble on the snake's body and injure it. Boas and King Snakes, among others, are usually good feeders.

Make your first snake one that is native to your area and is easily obtained. Read as much as you possibly can about local snakes and especially about how to tell a poisonous one from the harmless kind. Join a reptile club if there is one near you. Talk to the game warden or wildlife agent about where to find a snake.

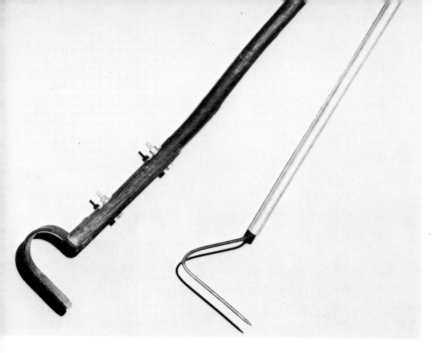

The equipment you need to catch a snake is a collecting bag, which can be a pillowcase or a cloth bag with a tight weave. It can be made of nylon, cotton, or a similar material that lets the air in but prevents the snake from escaping. Burlap is too loose, and the snake can wriggle right through it. You might also need a snake hook. A homemade one can consist of a three-foot stick with a metal right angle screwed tightly to one end, or you can buy a lighter and more versatile hook.

Spring is the best time to catch a small snake. A spot near a stream or pond is a good place to look. You might find the little Ring-Neck Snake, Garter Snake, or even the pretty Milk Snake curled up under a flat rock or on a sunny bank. Before you lift the rock, have the collecting bag handy. If the rock is very heavy, let someone lift it for you or use the snake hook to pull it up. Sometimes you can find quite a few little snakes curled up together. Take only one or two and let the others go free. You can pick up the small snakes by hand. They will seldom bite,

RING-NECK SNAKES   GARTER SNAKE AND RING-NECK SNAKES
RING-NECK SNAKE

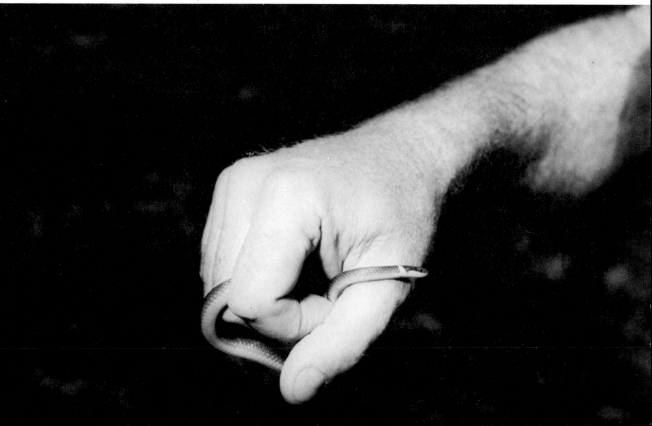

but they might empty their musk glands and release a bad-smelling fluid. Put the snake into the bag and tie or knot it securely. Always replace the rock exactly where it was in order not to destroy the habitat for the other snakes. Make sure that all the little snakes are out from under the rock before you let it slide back so you won't squash one. And watch your fingers.

If you want to catch a larger snake, pin it down gently with the snake hook and then grasp it directly behind the head. Hold it lightly, otherwise it will struggle too hard and hurt itself. Put it into the collecting bag at once. Some people with experience can scoop up a large snake with the hook without injuring it and transfer it to the bag.

Poisonous snakes should never be taken as pets. Don't leave the collecting bag with the snake inside in the hot sun for long. Get the snake into its new home as soon as possible.

The advantage of collecting a local snake is that if it refuses to eat and tame down, it can and should be released. But you must release it in the place where you captured it. If you do not, the animal will not survive, not even in a similar place.

A snake can also be purchased from a reputable reptile dealer. Those animals might have already adjusted to captivity and be eating regularly. Be sure to question the dealer about this. An animal that you purchase can never be released.

With snake-keeping, as with keeping any other pet, goes a great deal of responsibility for the life and well-being of the animal.

The home for a snake does not have to be very large, but it must be roomy enough for it to move about and stretch. It should not have any sharp edges, and it must be escape-proof.

There are plastic cages available in pet stores or at reptile dealers that are well suited for keeping a snake safe. They have a gliding glass front and are easy to clean and very light-weight. Another good home for a snake is a ten-gallon or larger glass aquarium that has a tight-fitting screen or small wire mesh top. Most pet stores sell them. A wooden cage with a glass front and screen top can also be used, providing the wood is splinter-free or painted with a nontoxic paint. Screening on the sides of the cage is not recommended since rubbing against it might injure the snake.

All snakes and the cages they live in must be kept dry. A water dish for drinking and soaking is all that is needed. Make sure that the water dish is heavy enough so that the snake cannot tip it over. The bottom of the cage can be covered with medium-sized, clean, and dry gravel or with newspaper. Newspaper might not look very attractive, but it is easily replaced when soiled.

FOX SNAKE

Snakes like to hide and will feel more secure and at home when a denlike place is provided for them. A curved piece of bark or a few flat stones arranged so that the snake can get underneath make a natural-looking habitat. A cardboard box of the size of a cigar box or tissue box, with a hole cut in one side, will be satisfactory for the smaller snakes. Larger snakes need roomier dens. A tree-climbing reptile needs a few twigs or branches to curl up on to be content. A water snake needs a bowl of water to get into, even if it is not large enough for swimming.

KING SNAKE

RAT SNAKE

44

RAT SNAKE

When you handle your pet snake, always support its body by letting it rest on your arm or hand. Don't pick it up by the tail and let it dangle.

Snakes should be kept at about 75° to 85°F. A 25-watt light bulb suspended over the cage will usually give off enough warmth for your pet. Very large cages might need a larger bulb. Check the temperature from time to time to make sure it stays the same.

Snakes are fascinating animals. Learning about their ways and accepting them for what they are will dispel all those unfounded fears and superstitions. We will see that they are an important part of our wild heritage and essential in keeping nature's balance.

INDEX

DISCARD

Page numbers printed in *italic* refer to photographs

Alta Community School District
Elementary Library